How to start and run your own computer repair business
By Joe Wisinski

Copyright 2011 - 2014 by Joe Wisinski

Introduction

You most likely bought this book because you're thinking about starting and running your own computer repair business.

Congratulations!

I was self-employed as a computer repair tech for more than nine years, and I found the business to be an excellent way to make very good income and call my own shots.

Like any endeavor, running your computer business has its joys and pleasures, as well as its pitfalls and problems. This book will tell you how to minimize the problems and maximize the pleasures of running your computer repair business.

Let's get started.

Advantages of running your own computer repair business

In my nine years as a self-employed computer repair tech, I learned there are a lot of advantages to being in this business. Here are some of them.

You work for yourself

You don't have a boss to tell you what hours to work, how to perform a particular job or anything else. That also means all the money you make is yours; you're not working so someone else can earn money.

You'll enjoy variety in your day

If you work as a self employed computer tech, you will enjoy a variety of work in your day. As an example, let me review for you what I did the day I wrote this. At my first appointment I taught a client who was having trouble using Microsoft Word. I also installed an anti-spyware program on his computer and ran a spyware check. I'll write more later about how little some clients know about computers and how you can make money by training them, but this is a good example of making money on training. My client had no idea what spyware is or why his computer needed to be free of it. At my second appointment I set up to a new printer and showed my client how to use it to print a few pictures. At my third appointment I replaced a bad power supply. At my final appointment of the day I installed a UPS (universal power supply). About a week earlier I had replaced a bad video card this computer. The card had apparently been destroyed in a power surge and I had explained to him how important it was to have a good surge protector on his computer system. As you know, it's not difficult to install a UPS; it's really just a matter of plugging it in. But many people don't know how to or don't want to be bothered with even the simplest computer-related tasks. That provides money-making opportunities for you.

After my four appointments I came home to work on a computer I had picked up from a client the day before. This computer had numerous virus and spyware infections, and overcoming the computer's many problems was a challenge, although an enjoyable one. As I write this, I am running another virus check on the machine to make sure I have completely rid the computer of all its viruses.

You see, then, that there was a lot of variety in my day. I also made quite a bit of money, not to mention the money I'll make when I return the computer that I'm working on now to my client.

You, too, can enjoy this kind of variety and interest in your day-to-day work.

You'll have no limit on income

I'll elaborate on this later, but for now, suffice it to say when you own your own business there's always ways to expand your services so that your income can get as high as you want.

You'll earn respect

To many people, computers are a vast mystery. Many people barely know how to turn the computer on and open a program. They greatly respect someone like you that can actually navigate through the computer's software and get the machine to do what they want, as well as crack open the case and replace parts. Add to that the fact that you know what to do when something goes wrong, and some people will look at you with something close to awe.

Is this business for you?

Not everyone is cut out to be their own boss. You should ask yourself these questions before making the leap from working for someone else to being self-employed.

Are you a self-starter? Can you motivate yourself? Can you handle problems as they arise? Are you wise enough to know that no one knows everything and are you willing to go to someone or some resource for help when necessary?

Are you a creative multi-tasker?

Can you go from teaching someone how to set up a spreadsheet to replacing a hard drive to discussing advertising rates with a sales representative, all within hours?

Are you able to handle the stress of not having a steady income?

Do you know what's it's like to get up in the morning without having income-producing work to do? Can you deal with that?

Do you know how to repair computers? Do you have a broad knowledge of hardware and software issues you'll face? Or if not, are you confident in your ability to learn how to repair computers?

Your answers to these questions don't all have to be "yes," but most of them should be if you're going to succeed in this business.

Before you even make the decision to become a self-employed computer technician, these are some matters you'll need to consider.

Where will you work from?

One of the first decisions that you have to make is where you will conduct your business from. I strongly recommend starting from your home. A spare room, or even part of a room, where you can set up a computer repair area will be fine. You really don't need a very large an area to work from, but because it's not always possible nor feasible to repair computers on clients' premises you do need some space at home, or somewhere, where you can repair computers. You'll need a desk to set computers on and some room for spare parts.

The setup I had at home was ideal, and you might want to emulate it. My computer repair area was in a spare bedroom of our house. My desk with my personal computer faced one wall. I had everything I needed for my personal time on that desk, including of course the computer itself, the monitor, a printer, a television, a DVD player, etc. This is where I spent most of my personal time. But right behind me, facing the opposite wall, was my computer repair desk. I had a monitor on the desk along with a keyboard and a mouse, so when I brought a computer tower home to repair it all I needed to do is plug it in and start working on it. As you probably know, when you work on a computer there's a lot of "down" time, when the computer is busy working but there's really nothing for you to do. For example, when the computer is running a virus check or you are reformatting the hard drive all you do is get the operation started and then let the computer do its thing. These operations take a long time and you don't need to be watching the computer every second while it's working. You do, however, need to baby sit operations in case anything goes wrong. So, while the computer I was repairing was working I could simply turn back to my own personal desk and continue with ever I was doing. Then on occasion I could turn around and see how the computer that I was repairing was doing. As I wrote this, in fact, I was checking a computer for spyware and viruses. Every few minutes I simply turned around to see if all was well with the computer I was working on.

This setup had obvious advantages for me, but also had an advantage for my clients. When a computer had more problems then I could easily resolve at the client's home, I told them that I wanted to take the computer home to work on. I told them, truthfully, that I could actually save them money by taking the computer home because I could be doing other things while the computer was working. This is good for client relations, because you're letting the customer know up front that you have their best interests in mind and you're trying to keep the cost of repairing their computer down as much as possible. The cardinal rule in this business is that you want happy and satisfied clients so that they will turn to you again when they need computer work and also will refer you to other people.

I recommend that you do *not* start with an office outside the home. Don't, for example, rent a storefront when you're first starting out. The reason should be obvious. Commercial space is expensive, and you simply won't make enough money at first to pay rent and make a go of your business. If you want to rent a storefront later, when your business starts to grow, that's fine. But don't overburden yourself with that expense at first.

As for computer hardware, you won't need much at your work area. Just have a monitor, mouse, keyboard and the necessary cables. With this hardware you won't need to take anything from your client's home or office to your work area except for the computer tower.

I like to have duplicates of tools in my home work area so I don't have to continually move the tools from my car to my office.

You can spend thousands of dollars on diagnostic equipment, but I don't think it's worth it. You should do just fine with the hardware I've mentioned.

Start part time

I cannot stress too strongly that you should start your business by working part time while holding on to your day job. Assuming you work a typical 40 hour a week job during the day, that leaves you the evenings and weekends to start your business. The reason I suggest starting part time is simply that it takes a long time to build up a client base. You can't jump into this business and expect to make a lot of money in the first few weeks. Service businesses don't work that way. You need time for people who see your advertisements to decide to call you, and to have you come to their home or business. No matter how much advertising you do, business doesn't come immediately. And remember that a prime way of getting business is through referrals, and that takes time. Furthermore, another huge part of your business is going to be repeat business. And again, it takes time to get repeat business. More than likely a client that you see this week will not need your services again for several weeks or months.

Now, if you happen to be in a position to live off your savings for a few months, or even up to a year or so, then you might consider jumping into business full time. But I don't recommend it. I think it's much better to start off part time, build your business, and gradually work up to full time work.

Be a trainer as well as a tech

Your business will involve both repairing computers and training people how to use them. Training lacks the challenge of repairing computers, and some technicians don't like the training aspects of the business. When you train people you have to be patient, you have to put yourself in their shoes, and you have to be willing to spend a lot of time with them on what to you seems a very simple procedure. Furthermore, you cannot be a computer "nerd" while training people. You have to speak to people in non-technical terms and easy-to-understand language.

Not everyone who knows about computers is a good computer trainer. In fact, it's difficult for people that know how to repair computers to be good trainers, because as a general rule our knowledge is far more advanced than the average computer user's knowledge and it's difficult for us to train people in very simple matters, such as how to save a word processing document.

But whether or not you like to train, it's going to be a big part of your business, even if you advertise yourself only as a computer tech. When you're at somebody's home to repair their computer, almost invariably they will ask you how to do some task on their machine. You just can't say, "I don't teach people how to use computers. I only fix them." You have to explain to them how to perform the task they're asking about. And indeed, you'd be foolish to not take the time to teach them, because most of the time, you're getting paid by the hour, and the longer you spend in the home or business, the more money you make.

I recommend that you do not advertise yourself only as someone who repairs computers. Your advertisements should reference the fact that you both repair computers and train people to use them. The reason for this is that I've found over the years that probably at least two times out of five when somebody responds to an advertisement they respond to the training part of the advertisement. They need to know how to do something on their computer, so they call me. I gain their trust as a trainer, and later, when their computer needs repairs they call me back to make that repair.

This matter of it not being easy for a lot of people to be a computer trainer can actually work in your favor. I can't tell you the number of times I've been to someone's home and had them say "My son, or my daughter, even or my husband or wife, knows all about computers. But they don't have the patience to teach me. They just sit here and go through it really fast and I don't learn anything." So, they call somebody that they think is going to be patient with them to help them learn to use the computer, and that someone can be you.

When you train people on how to use a computer, make it a hands-on experience for them. Don't sit in front of the computer with your hands on the keyboard or the mouse and show them how to perform a task. Let the person you're teaching sit in the chair and get their hands on the keyboard and mouse while you patiently tell them what to do. That's the only way they are going to learn.

And if they don't learn anything because you took over the computer from them, they will not have you back either as a trainer or as a technician.

What you'll need to get started

A reliable vehicle

You must have a vehicle that you're reasonably sure will get you where you're going. You don't want to break down on the way to an appointment, because that creates all kinds of problems, including the necessity of rescheduling not only the appointment you're on your way to but perhaps others, too. You might end up losing an appointment or two.

Your vehicle should also be one that will present the proper image to your clients. You don't want to show up in a junky clunker that you're embarrassed to drive; neither do you want to arrive in a high-end vehicle that most of your clients couldn't afford. People like to think that the person who comes to their home is "one of them," so go to your appointments in a middle-of-the-road, reliable vehicle.

Remember that you'll be doing a lot of driving, so it's good if your vehicle gets decent gas mileage.

Plenty of cell phone minutes

You'll be spending a lot of time on your phone, either making appointments or answering questions, so don't skimp on the amount of minutes on your monthly plan. It looks bad to not call a client back for hours because you had to wait until you got home to make a phone call so you could avoid using cell phone minutes.

Back in the days when I had a land line, I used to only give clients my cell phone number, never my home phone, because I didn't want them calling me at my home phone number. Alas, what sometimes happened is that people lost my business card and/or receipt, but remembered my name. They then looked up my home phone number in the phone book and called me at home anyway. I'm not sure there's much you can do about that, short of dumping your land line or not listing your home phone number in the book.

Business cards

One of the first purchases you'll make will be business cards. Don't skimp on your business cards. Get a good supply of high-quality ones. Remember that you'll be leaving your business card with clients and handing them out to prospective clients. You want to leave a good impression. That doesn't mean your cards have to be fancy. In fact, I discourage overly elaborate business cards. You want to draw attention to the services you offer, not to how beautiful your business card is. If you want to save on business cards a good place to order them is Vista Print (www.vistaprint.com). You can design your own card or use one of their templates.

My suggestion would be to put your business name (if any) your phone number, and the words "computer technician" on your card. You can also list "repairs," "upgrades," "new or used systems" and "training" as your services. Keep your card attractive without being ostentatious. Make sure it gives all the information clients or prospective clients need while at the same time being uncluttered and easy to read.

You'll also want your email address on your card, and I'd suggest you establish an e-mail address just for business purposes.

A business name

I always had my personal name, not a business name, on my business card. Yes, I had a business name and that's what I used formally, such as when the client made out the check and when I reported my income to the IRS. I left it off my business card, however, just to avoid clutter. My reasoning was that by the time I handed a client my card he or she already knew me by my first name and was, I hope, comfortable with me as a person. There's was no need for the business name and my conviction is that people are more at ease with a person than with a formal entity, such as a business. I also didn't normally put my business name in advertisements, for pretty much the same reason.

What you call your business is an important consideration. Keep it short (and thus easy to remember) but make it accurately describe your work. A common practice is to use the name or nickname of the area you live in along with "computer repair" or "computer service," that is "Astor Computer Services" or "Appalachian Mountains Computer Services." That works well, but there's a good chance one of your competitors has already named their business with that name and you can't duplicate an existing name.

Many people use their first name, or their last name if it's a simple one, along with "computer repair" or "computer service."

Some people come up with a clever name, often playing off the "geeky" image that computer techs have. You'll want to avoid that because such names imply that you're some kind of nerd who speaks in "computerese" and talks down to people.

Don't use a name that doesn't immediately make clear what kind of work you do, such as "Joe's Business Services" or "Joe's Enterprises."

Having a business name means some extra expenses, such as registering your name with your state and having a business bank account, but remember that you don't *have* to have a business name. You can do business just using your own name.

You may also need a business license. The requirements for a business license depend on where you live. There are uncountable thousands of cities, towns, townships, boroughs, etc. in the country, and it's impossible for me to list the requirements for every one. You should call your local governing authority or check their web site to find out what license you need, if any. If you need a license, chances are it will cost a relatively small amount of money per year.

You may wonder if you're allowed to run a computer repair business from your home. The answer is almost undoubtedly yes. Ordinances or regulations against running a home business are usually designed to prevent people from bringing a lot of vehicle or foot traffic to their home. That's not an issue in your type of business. Virtually 100 percent of your business will consist of you going to clients' homes; I can count on one hand with fingers left over the number of times in nine years a client came to my house.

Money

You won't need much money to get your own computer repair business going. Your biggest expense will be advertising. I can't tell you just how much money you need to get started because I don't know what advertising rates run in your part of the country or how much you are willing to spend on business cards. I also don't know what tools you may already own or will decide to buy. Neither can I tell you how many parts, or what parts, to have on hand as you start your business. For what it's worth, here's a rough rundown on what I spent in the first few weeks of running my business.

Business cards (in the pre order-your-cards-on-the-Internet days):$40

Advertising (one ad in a weekly newspaper): $20. But rates have gone up considerably since then. Because the ad was successful I spent more money in subsequent weeks for more advertisements, bringing my total ad expenditure in the first month to about $120.

Books to help me learn more about computer repair: $40. If you're already knowledgeable about computer repair you may not need to buy books.

Tools: $50. I already had a pretty good selection of tools, keeping my expenditure low.

Computer parts: $100

My approximate total expenditure for my first month in business, then, was about $350.

You see, then, that I didn't spend much money at all. But as I say, you may need to spend more or less, depending on your circumstances. Note that I already had the software I needed, so there was no expense there. But the real point here is that your start-up costs (assuming that you start part-time as I recommend) will be quite small. You're looking at hundreds of dollars at most, not thousands of dollars.

Tools

You will need some tools to perform your job properly. Fortunately, the tools you need are neither extensive nor expensive. Here is a rundown of the tools that you'll need.

You will need a couple of screwdrivers. The main one will be a medium size Phillips head screwdriver. Probably 90 percent of the time that's all you need to open a computer and take out a hard drive, CD drive, Ethernet card, or other part.

It's possible you may need a Torx screwdriver. Torx screws are five-slotted screws. You won't find a whole lot, but many Compaq computers used to be built using them. It's difficult to remove a Torx screw using a Phillips head screwdriver, so you might want to have a Torx screwdriver handy.

A flashlight sometimes comes in handy because lighting is often poor where you'll be working. You may find a free flashlight app for your cell phone that works for you.

I'd suggest you buy a multi-tester. As its name implies, a multi-tester allows you to conduct several tests. For example, if a computer is not getting power, you can check to see if there's voltage coming out of the wall socket and also check the computer's power supply to see if it's functioning.

I'd also suggest having a pair of channel lock pliers. I rarely used these, but sometimes they came in handy when pulling a stubborn power cord off a hard drive or CD drive. You can't exert a lot of force on the cable, but if the plug is sticking you can grab the cable with the pliers and gently rock it back and forth until it pulls loose.

If your close-up eyesight isn't top-notch, you might want a magnifying glass or a pair of reading glasses. Sometimes you'll need to read the fine print on motherboards or expansion cards.

Parts and supplies

I don't think it's necessary to carry around a lot of parts, but you do need some because it looks bad to the customer if you have to say, "I need to run to the store to buy a part." So carry at least one or two of the most used parts with you.

Otherwise, buy parts on as-needed basis so you don't have money tied up in excess inventory. What you'll need is a least one of every part that goes inside a computer., including a hard drive, sound card, video card, Ethernet card, power supply and a few memory chips. You'll want a few different size and type memory chips. Even then, however, because memory varies so much from computer to computer you'll find you can't carry every chip you may need.

You should also have an old hard drive for test purposes. If a computer's not booting and you suspect the hard drive might be bad you can disconnect the old drive and connect the new one. If the new drive boots up you've apparently found the problem.

It's also useful to have a spare monitor on hand. Occasionally a client's monitor will die and you can sell them one on the spot. Don't carry a monitor in your car, though. It's a hazard in case of accident.

If you have a laptop computer, great, but don't go buy one at this point just for your fledging business. A laptop is useful for diagnostic purposes. If a computer boots up okay but nothing is showing on its monitor, you can hook up the monitor to your laptop. If you then get a picture, you know the monitor is bad. If you don't get a picture, a good guess would be a bad video card in the computer.

You should have a selection of smaller parts, such as mice, keyboards, power cables and hard drive/CD drive cables. If you're at a client's house you can instantly sell him one of those parts for a quick profit.

When buying parts, remember that it's a perfectly acceptable and legitimate practice to mark up the cost when you sell them to your clients. For example, if you buy a new hard drive for $50 you're not going to sell it to your client for $50. You're going to charge the client a reasonable markup, maybe $70. You spent time and effort buying the part, which is time and effort that the client did not have to spend, even if he knew what to buy. But of course, nine times out of ten the client does not know what to buy, so you're also selling your expertise when you sell the part to your client. Your mechanic marks up the cost of parts when he fixes your car; you should too.

How much should you mark parts up? That's a question only you can answer. You know how much time you spent picking up the part and you know how much expertise it takes to buy it. It takes more knowledge to buy a video card than to buy a keyboard, for example, so logically you might mark the video card up by a greater percentage than you mark the keyboard up. You may also want to consider how much time you had to invest to get the part.

I made it a practice to buy parts as inexpensively as possible. Here's why: If I bought a part for say, $25, maybe I'd mark the part up to $35. But if I did some comparison shopping and bought that same part for $20, I could still charge my client $35, so I made more profit. Or here's another way to look at it: Say that through comparison shopping I bought the part that's normally $25 for $20. It's reasonable to make $10 profit on that part, so I'd sell it to my client for $30. If I hadn't done my comparison shopping and had bought the part for $25, I would have had to sell the part for $35 to make my $10 profit. So I charged the client $5 less, although my profit remained the same. Charging the customer less money made him happy, so I was more likely to get repeat business and referrals.

This doesn't mean I bought cheap parts; it just means I shopped wisely and tried to keep my costs down. Obviously, the Internet is a good place to buy parts inexpensively. Just don't get in the practice of buying poor quality parts online. Doing so will come back to bite you if the new part you installed only works for two months. I recall reading about one tech who said about 30 percent of parts he buys are bad. Apparently he bought poorly made parts. He must have wasted a lot of time switching parts in and out as he discovered they were bad and he must have had a lot of frustrated clients. It's not worth it. Buy good parts, but buy them as inexpensively as possible. I can't remember ever buying a part that turned out to be bad.

Software for your clients

You will need to have a selection of software both in your work area and to take to client's homes. This does *not* mean illegitimate copies of commercial software. It means free programs, which are readily available. What I did was copy the programs I needed on to a USB drive that I had with me at all times. (The USB drive was also useful for backing up client's files or moving the files to a new computer.) I also had the same programs on a couple of CDs. Here is a list of the programs I carried with me. I won't mention the programs by name because they may not be available when you read this, but there will be plenty of the following types of programs available for you.

An anti-virus program

Anti-spyware programs (I carried several different programs.)

A graphic-editing program

An office suite

A pop-up blocker

An unzipping program

Some of these programs come bundled with newer versions of Windows, but you might run across an older version of Windows without some of this software.

As software changes, you'll need to update this list, but you should find that this a good place to start. All of these programs can be found free online.

What technical knowledge you'll need

Obviously, to run a computer repair business you have to know how to repair computers. There are two aspects to computer repair, hardware and software. Let's take a look at these separately.

Knowledge of hardware

You'll need a good working knowledge of the hardware found in a typical desktop computer. You'll need to know how to physically replace a hard drive, memory, power supply, processor,

CD drives, and all expansion cards. Fortunately, it's not hard (in fact it's quite easy) to learn to replace computer hardware.

Teaching you how to repair computers is beyond the scope of this book, but I have two suggestions for you to learn how if you're not already a computer tech.

The first is to get yourself a couple of old computers, the kind where it won't matter if you make a mistake. You might find inexpensive computers at a thrift shop or a garage sale, or you might find somebody willing to donate an old computer or two to you. It doesn't matter too much if the computers are quite old. About the only changes to computer hardware in the years I was in the business was the change of memory type. When I started working on computers EDO memory was the standard memory; now you'll never see that type of memory any more. But even with memory, the basic technology, from the standpoint of a computer repair tech, is still the same - take the old chip out and plug the new chip in. It's not brain surgery.

Once you have a couple of old computers to work on, remove the case covers and start to poke around. Learn to identify the various parts of the computer. Buy or borrow a book on computer repair and thoroughly familiarize yourself with the computer's hardware. You want to get comfortable removing and replacing the various parts of the machine. One of the last things you want is to struggle in front of the customer with, say, physically putting a hard drive in. So practice until you're comfortable with computer hardware. I must point out, however, that even if you are thoroughly comfortable with replacing computer hardware sometimes this aspect of the work can be a little difficult. It's a funny thing, but the same geniuses who can design and build these incredibly complicated machines sometimes put memory in an inaccessible place, such as under a power supply. So what was supposed to be an "easy" addition of memory becomes a more difficult endeavor.

The second suggestion about learning to repair computers is to buy or borrow some good books on the topic. Here are a couple of books I recommend:

Upgrading and Repairing PCs, by Scott Mueller

This book is very comprehensive. It's not a book you'll sit down and just read through, but it's an invaluable reference tool.

Upgrading and Fixing PCs for Dummies, by Andy Rathbone

If you're new to repairing computers, this book is an excellent place to start learning.

Be sure to get the latest version of these books or any other ones you'll buy.

You'll also find it helpful to subscribe to one or more computer magazines. I found PC Magazine to be particularly useful.

What about A+ Certification? Should you get certified? For those who may not know, A+ Certification is the universally recognized standard of competence for computer repair technicians. A+ Certification shows you're knowledgeable about both software and hardware.

There are no particular requirements for testing for A+ Certification. You don't have to go to school, you don't have to have a certain number of years of experience, and you don't need to convince anyone that you can try to pass the A+ test. All you have to do is put your money down at a testing center and pass the test. (Currently it costs about $190 to take the A+ test.) Then you can legitimately call yourself A+ Certified. The question is, is it worth the money and the effort to pass the test? If you have any inclination to working for someone else then by all means you must have A+ Certification. But if your sole goal as a computer repair technician is self employment, then A+ Certification isn't necessary, although it's nice to have. In the more than nine years I was in business I never had a client or potential client ask me if I was A+ Certified. There's no doubt that few, if any, of my clients ever heard of A+ Certification, and they wouldn't have cared if I was A+ certified anyway. What computer owners want is someone to talk to them in language they can understand, and someone who can fix their computer at a reasonable cost.

See this web site for more information on A+ certification: www.comptia.org.

Software, and knowledge of software

You may know already that repairing computer hardware is the easy part. Nine times out of ten it's the software that will give you fits.

So in addition to knowing the hardware, you must know computer software well. There are uncountable thousands of computer programs, and no one can know them all. But you need a general knowledge of operating systems, browsers, word processing and spreadsheet programs and other commonly used software. You can't possibly know everything there is to know about software, but you'll find if you have a good basic knowledge of common programs, it's relatively easy to figure out how other programs work.

You will need to become very familiar with operating systems; not just one operating system, but several. Toward the end of my time in business Windows XP had been out for about five years and I suppose that probably about three-quarters of the computers I saw then had XP installed. Probably another 20 percent still had Windows 98 or 98SE as the operating system. The other five percent had Windows ME or Windows 2000. I can't tell you what operating system you'll need to know best because I don't know when you'll be reading this book. But Windows knowledge is critical to successfully running your business.

What about Macs? I didn't work on Macs because they are so different than Windows-based computers. With the current popularity of iPads you'll find it worthwhile to know Apple's iOS. There's no doubt that many of your potential clients own iPads, but don't know how to use them. And that's where you come in. You'll be able to make good money teaching people how to use their phones and tablets.

Now let's move on to the most critical part of getting your business up and running.

Advertising

You will find nothing more important to your success in the early weeks of your business than the decisions you make about advertising. The places you choose to advertise, the effectiveness of your advertisements, and the cost of the ads are all critically important to how much business you get in the early going. Let's break these down one by one.

You have many choices as to where to advertise. You have daily newspapers, weekly newspapers, the yellow pages, fliers, direct mail and more. Not only do you have many choices as to *where* to advertise, you have choices about the *type* of advertising, such as classified ads or display ads.

Here is what worked for me. Most communities are served by a weekly newspaper. (Weekly doesn't necessarily mean that it's published just once a week; it could be two or three times.) Typically, residents don't subscribe to these papers; they're often distributed to every home by being tossed onto lawns. They're also distributed through stands in front of grocery stores, shopping plazas, and other businesses. I placed by first ad in one of these papers and I advertised there for the entire time I ran the business. I started with a simple classified ad and used very much the same version of that classified ad for nine years. I'll discuss the ad I used in a moment so you'll get some ideas of what you should do. But I believe you can also learn by knowing what *not* to do, so first let's take a look at the advertisements of some of my competitors. Here are my thoughts on some of their ads.

The first one reads:

AAA ABSOLUTELY FREE In Home and Office Estimates. 23 yrs. of experience. Nine certifications. Call 555-1212.

I think this ad is a bit deceptive. For a start, the eye naturally goes to the words "absolutely free." But then the next line tells us that the only thing that's free are estimates. Big deal. Who doesn't give free estimates? Furthermore, notice the "AAA." That's obviously designed only to put this ad at the top of the list of alphabetical ads in the newspaper. AAA is not part of the business' name. It's just there as a blatant attempt to be first in line. Of course you want your ad to be at the top, but I don't think you should resort to such an obvious attempt to put your ad first. Remember that you want to establish a relationship based on trust with your clients. Bordering on deception right from the start is not the way to do so. The phrase "in home and office estimates" is fine, as is "23 years of experience." The "nine certifications" is a very bad idea indeed. Who cares how many certifications he has? Not the average client, for sure. I *never* had anyone ask me what certifications I hold. Stating that he holds nine certifications makes it look like this guy would speak way over the head of the average client, and I bet he would. In summary, then, I think this is a really poor ad. If I were a potential client looking for someone who wouldn't talk down to me, I would never call this technician. People who can't repair or use computers are looking for someone who doesn't speak over their heads.

The next ad reads:

AAA COMPUTER DOCTOR! 555 Main Street, Cooperstown. Repairs, Upgrades, Custom Builds (New and Used). In-home Service. Training. Credit Cards Accepted. Call 555-1212.

This ad is much better than the preceding one. This business is actually named "Computer Doctor," so he gets his business name in the ad. I still don't like the AAA, and again, it's not part of the business' name. Computer Doctor, though, is a great name for a computer tech business.

The ad then gives the address of the business (this is not a home-based business; he has a storefront in a good location on a busy road.) Then the ad clearly spells out what services the business offers. There is one problem, though. Training is listed as a service, but he lists it *after* stating that he offers in-home service. "Repairs, upgrades, custom builds, and training" are all services and should be listed together. It's fine to say he accepts credit cards, although in more than nine years in business I never had a client or potential client ask if I accepted credit cards. If I were starting again, however, I would accept credit cards, and I'd advertise that, too. You're probably aware of the excellent Square system for accepting credit cards. For any who may not be, Square will give you a free credit card reader for your smartphone. Customers simply swipe their card on the device and sign their name on your phone's screen. There's no upfront cost; Square takes a small percentage of the amount charged. For more about Square, go to squareup.com.

Overall, then, this is not too bad of an ad. I think the ad owner probably gets quite a bit of business from it. In fact, this ad has run for many years, and that proves it's successful.

The next ad reads:

COMPUTER SLOW? Acting Funny? In Home Computer Tune-ups, Repairs, Upgrades, Virus Cleansing. Call Bill at 555-1212.

This, I think, is quite a good ad. It starts by raising questions, which a potential client might answer by saying, "Yes, my computer is working slowly" and/or "It is acting funny." I'm not sure about the word "funny" though. Maybe "acting up" or "acting strange" would be better. Then the ad states that the service is in the client's home, which is important to many people, and the ad tells exactly what services the technician offers. This ad also mentions that tech's first name, and that's a nice personal touch. Remember that it's hard for some people to make a cold call to a phone number they see in an ad. Including your first name helps those people to pick up the phone and call you. The only thing this ad lacks, I think, is a reference to training.

Now the next ad:

FREE HARDWARE FIREWALL! Dust Off Your Old PC and Secure Your Data and Network. Call 555-1212

This ad is so bad it's incredible. To start, the word "hardware" will turn a lot of people off. Many computer users don't know what hardware is. They've heard the word, but don't know what it refers to. And then the word "firewall" is a terrible one to use in an ad. If many people don't know what hardware is, what do you think they know about a firewall? Most potential clients wouldn't have the slightest idea what a firewall is. And if people don't understand your ad you can be sure that they won't call you. The same goes for the words "data" and "network." And what does "dust off your old PC" mean, anyway? It sounds like the technician is suggesting that people get an old computer out of the attic and let him do something with it. And that's not what people want. This ad also includes a web site address. I can pretty much guarantee that no one goes to that site as a result of reading the ad. This technician is an obvious computer nerd who probably is hopeless when relating to non-nerd clients. Not coincidentally, I'm sure, this ad stopped running after a few weeks. No doubt the advertiser found the ad didn't work and therefore stopped running it.

The next ad reads:

IN HOUSE COMPUTER Services. Flat rate. No hourly charge. Free assessment. "We know stuff" Nerds Onsite, See our ad above the crossword puzzle. Call 555-1212

The phrase "in-house" is awkward here. I presume the author means "in-home." "In-house" generally means a service is performed by employees of a business rather than being contracted out. I think this technician is making a huge mistake by charging a flat rate for all services. There are many services that computer techs perform without possibly knowing how long they'll take. Virus removal is one. Does this guy really just charge a flat rate for removing viruses? That's hard to believe. If he does, he either has to charge a huge amount of money or he's working a lot of hours for little money. Either way is no good. If I was a potential client I'd shy away from this guy because I'd be thinking that his flat rate must be really high. I guess "free assessment" means "free estimate," but then, why didn't he say so? The phrase "we know stuff" is meaningless. Of course he knows stuff, presumably related to fixing computers. Why else would he be advertising for business if he doesn't "know stuff"? The word "nerds" is going to turn off a lot of people. Believe me on this one. The last thing people want is a nerd coming to their home to look at their computer. Instead, they want someone who will speak in simple, plain language that they will understand. The last part of the ad, which refers the reader to another ad, is okay. But if this ad was better written it wouldn't need to refer the reader anywhere else. This technician is spending money on two ads when one ad should do.

Finally, here is the ad I used the entire time I was in business, with great success:

IN-HOME Computer training and service. Patient teacher. Experienced technician. Reasonable rates. Satisfaction guaranteed. Joe. 555-1212

Note that, like a couple of my competitors' ads, I started with the phrase "in-home." This immediately told the reader that they got a benefit if they hired me - I would come to their house. Many people, especially those who know little about computers, don't want the hassle of unplugging all the cords and lugging their computer to a repair shop.

I have training listed first because I've learned that training is what most people are looking for. I didn't keep records on this, but as I said earlier, I think that probably at least two times out of five clients called me for training, rather than for service. Then later, when their computer needed servicing, they called me back because they liked me as a person and they liked how I taught them. I'm not sure I needed the word "computer" in my ad. The ad ran under the "computer services" heading, so it might have been redundant to speak about computer training. But I left the word computer in just so it was perfectly clear that was what I was talking about. After listing training first, then I mentioned service. I didn't go into details about what kind of service because most people just do not know what kind of service their computer needs. They only know their computer isn't working as it should.

Now, the next two words are the most important in the ad, especially the word "patient." I can't tell you how many times clients told me the reason they called me instead of a competitor was the word "patient." They always said the same thing. "I'm computer illiterate and I need someone to be patient with me." I wrote "experienced technician" just to try to reassure prospective clients that I really did know what I was doing. Think about it for a moment. When you call someone for a service isn't there a slight amount of doubt in your mind, wondering if the repairman really knows his job? I stuck "reasonable rates" in the ad because another fear that people have is that they will get soaked by the repair person. And "satisfaction guaranteed" assures people that if they weren't happy with my service they wouldn't have to pay. (I never had it happen, though, that I didn't get paid for a job because the client wasn't happy with my work.) Finally, notice that I mentioned my name. As I said earlier, that helps people who may be reluctant to pick up the phone and call. Notice that the whole ad is simple to read and understand. I used short, easy-to-understand words and phrases.

All the ads above, including mine, were classified ads. When you run a classified ad you generally get a certain number of words included in the cost of the ad, typically 15 to 20 words. If you exceed that number you pay for each extra word. The additional cost can add up quickly, so try to keep your ad right at the number of words you get for the flat rate. The publication I used gave me 15 words for the base cost. My ad ran 16 words, but I paid for that extra word each week because the ad worked well as written.

What makes a good ad?

Now let's look a little deeper at what makes a good ad. Specifically, I want to talk about the importance of showing *benefits,* not just *features* in your ad. Here's the difference - a feature is simply a description of an item, while a benefit shows what the consumer will get because he or she uses that item. For example, say you're looking at a new computer. You see that it has eight gigabytes of RAM and a 500 gigabyte hard drive. Those are *features*. They merely state what the computer has. What you are interested in is the *benefits* you get because of those features. What you need to know if you're going to buy that computer is that 8 gigabytes of RAM allows you to have many programs open at once, and the 500GB hard drive means you have plenty of storage space. Those are the benefits. So, when you write your advertisement make sure the reader will see the *benefits* of hiring you, not merely a description of what you offer.

Let's look at my ad again as an example of the difference between features and benefits.

IN-HOME Computer training and service. Patient teacher. Experienced technician. Reasonable rates. Satisfaction guaranteed. Joe 555-1212

Did I show benefits, and not just features? Well, my ad was a mixture of benefits and features. "In home," "reasonable rates," and "satisfaction guaranteed" are benefits for the potential client, but "patient teacher" and "experienced technician" are really features more than benefits. The benefit for a potential client when I said that I'm patient was that I wasn't going to show exasperation if she didn't understand a concept immediately. But, I couldn't very well write all that in my advertisement, so I just said "patient teacher." Potential clients knew what the benefit of my patience was for them. Similarly, the benefit of my being an experienced computer tech was that I'd be unlikely to damage a system in the process of fixing it. Again, I couldn't say all that in an advertisement, but the potential customer understood what I meant.

It's not easy to write an ad consisting entirely of benefits. But try. You'll get more business if a potential client sees how you can benefit him instead of just seeing a listing of the services you offer.

Now, let's continue thinking about what types of ads work. As I mentioned, I found classified ads in the local weekly paper to be a great source of business. Logically then, if a classified ad works then a display ad should work better, right? That's what I thought. So I once tried placing a display ad in the same newspaper. The results were terrible. That ad was the only ad I ever published that got me no business whatsoever. It seemed logical to me that if a small ad brought business, then a larger ad should have brought at least as much business and perhaps more. But it didn't work out that way.

I tell that story to make a point about advertising. Advertising is very much an art, not a science. What works for me may not work for you. What works this week may not work next week. What works in one part of the country may not work in another part of the country. All my suggestions about advertising are meant to be guidelines, not absolute rules.

Final thoughts about writing your ad

If you're not confident of your ability to write a good advertisement, get some help with it. You don't necessarily have to pay a professional to write your ad. Ask a friend or your spouse to help you. I can't overstress the importance of a good ad. Your business won't be successful without one.

And, by the way, keep your advertising, like all parts of your business, professional. Don't, for example, stick up a hand-lettered sign on a telephone pole to advertise your business. Think of it this way - would *you* call someone who advertised their business in such as amateurish way? Make sure you can be justifiably proud about the way you tell the world about your work.

How much will ads cost?

Let's talk about the cost of advertising. In advertising, the critical dollar figure is called *cost per thousand*. In other words, you want to know how much your ad will cost for every 1,000 people it reaches. So if your ad costs $10 and reaches 1,000 people, that means it costs one cent for every person you're reaching. To get the cost per thousand, you simply divide the cost of your ad by the number of people it reaches, and then multiply by 1,000.

As you see then, figuring cost per thousand is quite easy. In practical terms, however, it's much more difficult to determine your cost for reaching a certain number of potential clients. This is because it's really not possible to know how many people your ad is reaching. All you can really know is the *circulation* of the publication that your advertising is in. You really don't know how many people actually *read* that publication, and more importantly, you don't know how many people read your ad.

Publishers of newspapers and magazines will tell you that a certain number of people read each copy of their publication. This is called the *readership number*. Usually when publishers say "X number of people read our publication," what they're figuring is that anywhere from two to three people read each copy of the publication. But keep in mind that publishers have a vested interest in keeping the readership figure high, because the more people read their publication, the more money they can charge for advertising. So be skeptical about readership figures supplied by the publisher. I think the best you can do is look at actual publication figures. That's the number of copies that are actually printed.

When I left the business, my advertisement in the weekly newspaper cost $32.50 a week and went into about 100,000 newspapers. My cost per thousand then, in circulation, not necessarily in readership, was 32 1/2 cents. That is a figure I can work with because, theoretically, I could compare that cost per thousand for this publication with other publications and see where the best advertising deal is.

If only it were that simple. There's another factor that figures in, and that's the quality of the publication. What do people think of the publication you're thinking of advertising in? Is it respected? Are people reading the publication for its content, or just for its advertising? That makes it a great deal of difference.

I've tried advertising and many other publications besides the weekly newspaper, including flyers that come in the mail and advertising flyers that people pick up in grocery stores, post offices, and department stores. Sometimes the cost per thousand was less then the newspaper, but the response was less too.

So you see that it's not easy to determine where the best place to advertise is because there are too many unknowns and variables. Here is a good rule of thumb though - advertise where affluent people are most likely to see your ads. You want to get clients for whom money is no object. You don't want people who complain about the cost of your service call, or worse, can't even afford your service to begin with. You want people who can easily afford to pay you and keep you coming back for more service on their computer. Sometimes a potential new client would call me and ask me what I charged. Occasionally, their immediate response was something like "you charge way too much" followed by the hanging up of a phone in my ear. That's unpleasant, but I really didn't mind too much because someone who's overly concerned about cost isn't the type of client I wanted anyway.

I also had clients or potential clients who didn't want to pay me my minimum time, which was one hour. I had people ask, "Can you come to my house for 20 minutes?" What they wanted, of course, was to pay me just one-third of my usual hourly rate. I always told them, "I'm sorry, I don't do that." You can't make a living that way and you don't want clients like that.

Advertising online

What about advertising online? If you can find a web site that targets local residents you might check it out. I'm skeptical about the viability of online ads for this reason - the people who will seek your services, as a whole, don't know much about using computers. That's why they need you. They probably don't have the knowledge to seek out your services online. If you already have a web site, you'll of course advertise your services, but I strongly recommend that you stay away from pay-per-click ads that run on other web sites, at least at this point in the life of your business. You can quickly burn through a ton of money with pay-per-click ads.

Consider a newsletter

Now let's talk about another advertising method. You'll find this information extremely valuable for getting repeat business and referrals. I suggest you periodically send a newsletter to your current clients. I couldn't tell you how well this practice worked out for me. Sometimes clients I hadn't heard from in months, or even years, would call and when I go to their home I'd see my newsletter by their computer. They would tell me, "I lost your business card, but I got your number from the newsletter." Other people told me, "I really enjoy your newsletter." Reading between the lines, that means those people will remember me the next time they call for computer service.

The newsletter I sent was *not* a hard-sell advertisement. It was information I thought my clients would find useful, presented in easy-to-understand terms.

Sending the newsletter was a fairly expensive proposition. When I was in business, stamps cost 39 cents each. I wrote and laid out the newsletter myself and copied it at a local office supply store. Copies then ran 8.5 cents for one double-sided page, plus seven percent tax, for a total of about 9 cents per copy. I sent out one double-sided page in an envelope, with the envelopes costing a penny each. So if you do the math, this is what you get:

Stamps: 39 cents

Copies: 09 cents

Envelopes: 01 cent

So the cost for each copy of the newsletter I mailed was 49 cents.

It cost me, then, about $49 for every 100 copies of the newsletter I sent. But it was worth every nickel, and much more, even though it took me almost a whole day to write, copy, add addresses, fold, stuff, and take the newsletter to the post office. The newsletter more than paid for itself each month. Once you get a large enough customer base to make it worthwhile, I highly recommend that you send a newsletter to your clients. You don't have to be a great writer. Just share good information with your clients in an easy-to-understand way, just like you do when you're talking to them.

I didn't send the newsletter to every client. Before taking the newsletter to the copy shop I went through my client list and chose who would get the newsletter. For numerous reasons, I weeded out some clients. Maybe they mentioned that they'd soon be moving out of my service area, or perhaps they were quite knowledgeable about computers and wouldn't be interested in the relatively simple information I included in the newsletter. You'll want to use a "rifle" approach when sending the newsletter, not a "shotgun" approach. Save yourself some money by only targeting those you think are most likely to want and need your services again.

Customer relations

Few matters are more important to the success of your business than the relationship you maintain with your customers. You've heard the old saying "the customer is always right." I don't really think that is the case. People are not always easy to get along with and sometimes the customer is wrong. But the customer is always the customer, and if you want your business to succeed you must know how to get along well with the people who write out checks to your name.

Keep in mind that the people you deal with every day are your livelihood. Treat them with the platinum rule in mind. What is the platinum rule? The platinum rule says to treat other people as they want and expect to be treated.

Here are some day-to-day situations that will arise with your customers and how to handle them.

Telephone calls

Almost always, your first contact with potential clients will be by telephone. Because you'll be spending a lot of time on the phone, a good manner is essential. Answer the phone in a friendly way. There's a saying, "a smile can be heard," meaning that if you're smiling while on the phone the person you're talking to can tell you're upbeat and friendly. So smile as you're answering the phone. Don't just say, "Hello." Say, "Hi, this is Sam," or, if you prefer, "Hi, this is Sunshine Computer Repair." It doesn't hurt to also say something like, "How can I help you?" People appreciate that.

You should be aware of this unfortunate reality about the telephone: People will call you at all hours of the day and night. I had people call me as early as 7 a.m. and as late as 10 p.m. I even had people call me after 9 on a Sunday night. Why people called at that time was a mystery to me. Would it have made any difference if they had waited another 12 hours and called me Monday morning during normal business hours?

I tried to answer the phone if possible instead of letting voice mail pick up. Answering the phone rather than let voice mail pick it up is good business. Obviously, if I was at someone's home or business I couldn't answer the phone and talk to someone else while the first person was paying me by the hour. I always had my phone with me though in case of emergency; with the ringer set on vibrate.

I did make one exception to answering phone calls. Sunday was the one day of the week I usually didn't work, and I made it a practice to not answer the phone on Sundays. My philosophy was if I answer the phone on a Sunday I'm only encouraging that person to call me back on another Sunday. To the best of my knowledge I've never lost business by not answering the phone on Sundays. As it happens, I'm writing this on a Monday, and yesterday I received three phone calls, two from current clients and one from a new client. In keeping with my practice, I didn't answer my phone because it was Sunday, but I returned the calls first thing Monday morning. I was able to reach two of the three people who called, and made appointments with both. The third person merely had a question he wanted answered over the phone, and I did my best to answer that question in the message I left. So you see that not answering the phone on Sunday didn't hurt my business.

When you can't answer the phone, either because you're with a client or otherwise engaged, be sure to return calls in a timely manner. Most people have no problem with waiting a few hours for your return call; most don't even mind if you wait until the next day. But don't leave people waiting for days before you call them back. That's not good business.

You'll find that some clients won't leave you a description of what the issue is when they leave a voice mail. They'll just say, "This is John Jones. Please call me at 555-1212." I always thought that was a little odd and it certainly isn't helpful. It's much more useful when people tell you what the problem or issue is so you can be thinking about it before you return their call.

One final point about phone calls: If you're going on vacation or otherwise can't or won't be answering calls, be sure to change the greeting on your phone to let people know you won't be returning calls for a few days. You don't have to say you're on vacation if you prefer not to. Simply say something like, "Hi, this is computer technician Bill Smith. I'll be out of town and unavailable until Monday, May 19. Please leave a message and I'll call you back then. Thank you."

I never, to the best of my knowledge, lost an appointment because of being on vacation. People understand that you have a life, too. In fact, clients almost always asked me how my vacation was or said, "I hope you had a good vacation" when I returned their calls after I got back.

And by the way, make sure you do take a yearly vacation. You need the time off and you'll be a better businessperson if you get away for a while. Sure, you'll be extra busy when you get back, doing current calls as well as the ones you missed while gone, but that's fine. Having the time off is worth it.

Making appointments

As I said earlier, almost all your appointments will come over the phone. The exceptions are an occasional time when you meet someone out in public, either a current client or someone you're introduced to. Or sometimes a current client will e-mail you to set up an appointment.

No matter how a client contacts you, when you set a time to meet them at their home or office, there are two practices you should avoid. One is telling people something like, "I'll be there between 8 and 12." Don't give people an hours-long range of when you'll arrive. Give them an exact time. Your clients have lives, too, and they don't want to have to hang around their home or business waiting for you to show up. You no doubt have gone through the "We'll be there between 1 and 5 routine," when you've called other service businesses. You know how that throws your day off, so don't do the same to your clients.

The other practice to avoid is *telling* people what time you're going to arrive. *Ask* them instead. Say something like, "How is 10 for you?" or "Does 1 p.m. work for you?" You shouldn't assume that the time that's convenient for you is the time that's convenient for your clients. They are the customers; they are the ones paying you, and you should make appointments at times that are convenient for them.

As you make your appointments, you should have a place to write them down so you don't forget where you're going and when. For years I used to write my appointments on small scraps of paper and stuff the paper in my pocket or put it on my car seat. The snag with this method was that sometimes I'd misplace the papers and have to call the client back to get their address. And even though I was pretty good at remembering where I was going and when, still on occasion I'd schedule conflicting appointments because of not having a list of all my appointments in front of me when I got a call.

I found a far better system when I started entering all appointments in my phone. Everything I needed was in one place and of course I always have my phone with me.

Be there on time. Or call

Just as clients don't want you to give them the "I'll be there between 1 and 5" routine, neither do they want to sit and wait if you're going to be late. So be on time, or call if you're going to be more than just a few minutes late.

My practice was to call the client if I was going to be more than five minutes late, whether it was because an earlier appointment ran longer than expected or traffic was heavy. Whatever the reason, it's good customer relations to call and let the client know if you're going to be late. But, again, do your best to be on time. I had numerous clients say, "You're right on time. I like that." Being on time shows your clients you're concerned about them.

But there's another part to this advice about being on time. Sometimes things work out so that you will be getting to a client's home early. What do you do then? It's just as important to not get to a client's home early as to not get there late. If you show up early the client may be busy, they may be eating lunch, or they may still be in the shower. So try to be at your appointments right on time, neither late nor early. There will be the occasional time when you have to kill a few minutes in order to not be early to an appointment. And that's okay. You can always find something to do for a few minutes, like stop and use a restroom, buy yourself a drink, or read a book or newspaper for a few minutes.

And speaking of restrooms, this may sound a little crude and I don't mean it to be, but sometimes you'll find yourself in need of the restroom while at a client's home. That's fine. Whenever I asked a client if I could use their restroom the response was always a gracious, "Of course. It's down the hall, the last door on the left." But the situation I tried to avoid was having to use the restroom within the first few minutes of meeting a new client. That doesn't look the best. You just walk into the house to meet the person and to work on their computer, and you're asking to use the restroom. To me, it just doesn't look so good. I tried to use the restroom on the way to an appointment instead of having to use it soon after I got to somebody's house. And one final word on the subject of using the restroom. Try to only do so while waiting for a computer to do something, even if it's just to start up after rebooting. In other words, don't stop in the middle of a task and ask to use the restroom. The reason should be obvious. People are paying you a lot of money per hour and you don't want them to feel taken advantage of. It's not too much to ask to wait a few minutes until you get to what is, in effect, a stopping place to use the restroom. It's much better to say, "It's going to take a few minutes for the anti-spyware program to run. Meanwhile, do you mind if I use your restroom?" than to run down the hall in the middle of some task. You don't want your clients to think they're paying you to use the restroom.

Even in this day of GPSs, sometimes you'll find that you have a hard time finding a new client's home. Don't hesitate to call and explain. You will find people are very understanding and helpful. I even had people stand out in their front yard and wave as I drove by to get my attention when I had a hard time figuring out which house was theirs. It is, after all, to the client's benefit to get you there so you can fix their computer.

Dealing with people in their homes or businesses

I mentioned earlier that a good phone manner is important, and a good manner with people in their homes is just as important, if not more so. You've probably had the experience of doing business in your home with someone who apparently couldn't care less about you. Perhaps they were surly, sloppy, unfriendly, or just indifferent. You may have even wondered, "Why am I giving my money to this person?" You don't want your clients to have the same thoughts. Remember, you want repeat business and referrals, so here are a few tips for dealing with clients as you meet them and enter their home or place of business.

As the person you're meeting opens the door, smile, look them in the eye and say, "Hi, I'm Fred Smith, the computer tech." Don't hold your hand out for a handshake, but if they hold out their hand, shake it firmly, but briefly, while you look them in the eye.

Usually people will say, "Come on in." When they do, say, "Thank you" because a person's home is his or her castle and they're inviting you into it.

If you live in a climate with snow, knock the snow off your shoes or take your boots off before entering the home.

Don't be assertive about walking through a client's home, even if you've been there before and know where the computer is. Let them lead the way. People don't want to feel that you're invading their property.

You'll find many people make small talk about the weather or current events to break the ice when they meet you, and that's fine. Converse briefly with them, but don't waste a lot of time before getting down to business. Remember people are paying you a lot of money, so don't waste a lot of their time in chit-chat. You can even begin looking over their computer system as you're pleasantly chatting with the client.

Call people by their names as you're talking to them. People like to hear the sound of their names. Don't sound like a used car salesman though, as in "Mike, I think you have some spyware on this computer. I should be able to take care of that problem, Mike."

You might wonder if some people resent being called by their first names. Maybe. I had potential clients call and say, "This is Mrs. Jones," as if that's how they expect to be addressed. I even had cases where someone didn't even tell me their first name when I got to their homes. On a few occasions, I had to politely ask, "What's your first name?" Then I addressed them by that name. I never had any indication that someone didn't like me addressing them in this manner. I had medical doctors and PhDs as clients. I also had a lot of clients in their 80s. No one seemed to mind my calling them by their first name. The only exception I can think of is if you're very young. Then you might consider the additional formality of addressing people who are middle-aged or older, or those who hold prestigious positions, as Mr. or Mrs. But even then, I think in most cases you'll find people will say, "Call me Mike."

One thing you may not like is that almost all clients will sit right next to you while you work on their computer. I don't know why people do this. Do they stand next to the plumber as he works? Do they sit nearby while the TV repairman does his job? I don't know, but I do know that probably 95 percent of my computer clients sat right next to me. Furthermore, a lot of them talked while I was trying to analyze what was going on with their computer. That would have been okay if what they were talking about was just what their computer was doing. But usually they didn't. They talked endlessly about various and sundry other topics while I was trying to figure out what was happening with their computer and what I could do to resolve the problem, and that was sometimes distracting. You don't want to ignore your clients or be rude as they're talking, but at the same time you often need to concentrate on the task at hand, and people don't always make it easy to do that.

Worse yet are those who grab a bite to eat or drink and sit there chomping or slurping while you're working. Yes, some people can be very rude. To be fair, most people that grab a bite or a drink will ask if you want something. Try to accept; you'll enjoy some excellent refreshments while working. A number of times clients even asked me to stay for lunch and I always enjoyed that.

Occasionally a client may ask if you want an alcoholic beverage while you're working, usually a beer. You should always politely decline with a "no, thank you," for two reasons: The first is that you're working. How many people do you know who drink while on the job? Furthermore, once you're done at that client's home you'll have to drive to another client's. You really don't want to drink and drive, not even just one beer. I strongly recommend that you decline any such offers.

However, clients will also offer you many good things. Many clients gave me small gifts, such as home grown fruit or vegetables. Sometimes people will give you their old computers or computer parts.

Dress to impress

How should you dress for your appointments? In a word, well. You should look decent and professional without looking ostentatious. Don't wear shorts. Don't wear jeans. Don't wear a t-shirt. For men, wear dress pants and a nice shirt with a collar. Tuck your shirt into your pants. Wear comfortable dress or casual shoes, not sneakers. For women, slacks are fine, with either a pullover shirt or a blouse. Don't wear high heels. Women should dress modestly. I won't try to define what "modestly" is because the definition varies widely, but don't call attention to yourself.

I don't think it's necessary for men to wear a tie, but I've noted with interest that some of the nationwide computer tech services do require their employees to wear them.

You should dress well for two reasons. The first reason goes back to the point I've often made in this book and will continue to make. Your clients are your livelihood and you *must* make them happy and keep them happy. Most people don't appreciate someone coming to their home dressed shabbily. They want and expect you to look like the professional you are.

A second reason why you should dress well is that the way you dress is a reflection of your own attitude toward yourself and your job. Dressing professionally shows that you consider yourself a professional. You'll feel better about yourself and do a better job if your dress the part. Your job is not a dirty one and there's no excuse for looking sloppy. Look like someone that you'd want to invite into your home.

Keep your terminology simple

As you explain what's wrong with someone's computer and what you're going to do to fix it, you'll find that most people have no idea what you mean. That's not a reflection on their intelligence or on your ability to express yourself; it just means computers are complicated machines that many people have a hard time understanding. So, when you're explaining keep it as simple as possible. Use analogies that your clients can relate to, such as "Think of the computer's hard drive as a storage cabinet. All the information in the computer is stored on the hard drive." And yes, I know that technically speaking, some information, such as the computer's date and time, is stored on the CMOS. Don't even try to go there with your clients. That information will be way beyond their understanding.

People don't like it when you talk down to them or when you speak over their heads. They'll appreciate it if you try to explain what's going on with their computer in simple terms.

Leaving on good terms

As I've said many times, repeat business and referrals are your goals. One way to ensure repeat business is to impress clients with your courtesy, so always be sure to say "thank you" to customers as you leave their home or office. I usually said thank you as they were handing me the check. Think about this from the client's standpoint. They've just given you some of their hard-earned money, perhaps a substantial amount of money. They expect a gesture from you in response, so make sure to say thank you.

Having said that, however, I should also note that virtually all the time, clients will say "thank you" to *you*. They really appreciate your fixing their computer. However, that does not mitigate the necessity of you also saying thank you to them.

One more thought about the check. You want to make sure that it is filled out completely and accurately, including having the right date, your name or the name of your business, the dollar amount (both in numerals and written out) and a signature. The problem is, you don't want to be obvious about doing this because that doesn't look good. So try to unobtrusively glance at the check as you're putting it away to ensure all information is accurate. Often the client will turn away briefly and you can get a good look at the check then. The reason for making sure the check is right is that it can be embarrassing for the client if you have to go back the next day to get a corrected check, not to mention it's a waste of your time.

You should leave receipts with clients, with a copy for yourself. A receipt carries several advantages. For you, receipts help keep track of clients' names, addresses, phone numbers and when you were at their homes, along with the work you did for them. Later on I'll tell you how to set up a spreadsheet to keep track of this information, and more, but a receipt gives you a backup hard copy.

For clients, the receipt gives them assurance that you'll not try to come back and collect money later. They have tangible proof, without waiting for their check to clear, that they paid you. This is especially important if they paid in cash, which will happen with about 10 percent of your clients.

And most importantly, the receipt gives another place for your clients to go to find your phone number when they need to call you for another appointment.

The receipt doesn't have to be fancy. You just need your name, or business name if you have one, your phone number, a place for the client's name, the date you performed the service and a brief description of what you did, along with the charge for that day's work.

You have several choices for the receipts that you use. One, you can buy a receipt book. The advantage to buying a receipt book is that everything you need, including the carbon copy, is there. But the disadvantage is you'll have to write your name and phone number on each receipt, and that doesn't look professional. Two, you can print receipts from your computer. The advantage is you can design the exact receipt you want and make it look very professional. The disadvantage is if you print on a laser or inkjet printer, you won't have a copy for yourself, although that may not matter to you if you keep all your records electronically.

The third option is to have your receipts professionally printed. A printer can print a superb-looking receipt, along with its carbon copy. The obvious disadvantage is this is the most expensive option.

One final note about your relationship with clients: I had quite a few clients who I also considered personal friends. There was one man who was one of my first clients and we became good enough friends to go golfing and out to dinner together. I also had clients that I started working for when I first started the business and was still working for nine years later. Developing a personal relationship with clients is almost always a positive thing. Having good friends is one of the great joys in life, and frankly, it's good for business too. The one caveat - if, for example, you're a married man and your client is a single woman; well, you know where I'm going there; there's no need to elaborate.

Difficult situations

You can look at your work in this way: you're not in the *computer* business; you're in the *people* business. And because you're dealing with people, you're going to have problems. Here's how to handle some of the most common ones.

Clients asking for advice over the phone

You will invariably find that some of your clients will call you up for "just a quick question." Fortunately, this will be a small portion of your clientele, perhaps 10 to 15 percent. But the question is, how do you handle them? One option it is to say, "I'm sorry, but I can't answer questions over the phone." The problem with that approach is that you have probably lost that person as a customer forever. So that's not a good option. A much better approach is to do your best to answer their questions. This can be difficult, for a couple of reasons. One is that people have a difficult time explaining their computer problems, especially over the phone. I once had a man call me and say. "My TV's working but I can't get on the Internet." I couldn't figure out what his television had to do with his Internet access - I knew he didn't have Web TV - and it took me a few seconds to realize what he was talking about. He meant the computer monitor was working okay but he couldn't access the Internet. He didn't know the terminology and called the computer monitor a TV. And that was a very simple issue. Imagine what happens when people get into the more esoteric operations of a computer. So for you, the computer tech, it can be very frustrated dealing with people over the phone. In the back of your mind you know that you could probably solve the issue immediately if you could only be there in person. But you can't, because someone is hoping to save money by getting you to answer their question for free on the phone.

What I did when I couldn't easily solve a problem over the phone is to suggest I come out in person. I usually said something like, "This problem could be caused by a number of issues. I won't be able to solve the problem unless I look at the computer in person." Or, "It's very difficult for me to say without having your computer in front of me. Would you like to me to come to your house to take a look at it?" Almost always people were willing to let me come to their house for a paid call. One reason they were was they knew I was doing them a favor by trying to answer their question over the phone, and that helped lower their resistance to letting me come to the house for paid service call.

Although it is true that many companies charge for technical support on the phone, as a practical matter it would be hard to get clients to pay you, the independent computer tech, for this type of support. Furthermore, offering phone support alone, without service calls at your clients' homes, is doing them a disservice. This is because when you visit somebody in their home invariably you'll find work that needs to be done on the computer or questions that the client may have about operating the computer. It's much better, both for you and for the client, to actually visit the client at their home or business and work on their computer there.

Another problem with answering questions over the phone is that a certain percentage of people will try to take advantage of your generosity. They will call you repeatedly to ask you questions. At some point you may need to tell a few people "I'm sorry, I can no longer answer questions over the phone." I only had to do that a few times. I didn't want to lose these people as clients, but I did have to draw the line as far as helping them over the phone. So what I did was tell them that I was no longer able to answer *any* questions over the phone, rather than saying I couldn't answer *their* questions over the phone. I let them think that not being able to take phone questions from anyone any more was a new policy on my part, rather than making them think I was singling them out. That strategy worked. Of the three people I had to tell this to, two remained my clients.

As a general rule, though, you want to answer as many questions over the phone as you can. You will find that people genuinely appreciate your help and therefore are more willing to call you back to their homes again for a paid service call. Simply put, answering questions over the phone, as long as it does not go to an extreme, is good business practice. A few minutes invested in a phone call may pay off in more business down the road. Remember too, that if people are happy with your service, including your willingness to try to help them over the phone at no charge, then they are more willing to refer you to other people. And referrals are the best way to get new clients.

At times, you'll be astounded at the simplicity of some the questions people ask you on the phone, and in their homes, too. I had people call and say to me after I'd been to their home, "When I start my computer it beeps once. I don't remember it doing that before. Is that okay?"

What do you say to a question like that? All you can do is smile to yourself and say, "Yes, that's fine; it's normal for the computer to beep once." When you get less-than-intelligent questions, whether on the phone or at a client's home or business, you just have to bear with it. You just can't do or say anything that would make the client think their question is a dumb one, not if you want to keep that person as a client.

Canceled calls

Another difficult situation to deal with is when you have an appointment set with a client, and he or she calls to cancel.

You have probably made appointments with professional people such as doctors and been told that if you fail to show for your appointment without calling to cancel at least 24 or 48 hours before the appointment you will be charged for the time. That's quite common among professionals. Should you have a policy like this in your business? I think it's a bad idea. Remember that you are after repeat business and referrals. If you tried to charge someone because they did not cancel their appointment within a specified period of time, what do you think the chances are of that person setting another appointment with you or referring you to another potential client? They won't do it. The much better idea when someone calls to cancel is to simply accept the cancellation in good grace. Usually people will apologize and you should reply with something like "That's quite all right. No problem at all. I understand things come up." Of course, the truth is it's not really all right. You set aside time for that person, you've arranged your schedule to include that call, and now they've disrupted your day. You may even have been counting on the income you would have received from that appointment. Now it's gone and that's not a pleasant situation. But it's much better to keep the client's goodwill by cheerfully telling them it's no problem that they had to cancel.

Furthermore, as a practical matter, say you did try to charge a client for canceling an appointment. What do you think the chances are of actually collecting the money? I would be optimistic if I said slim to none. Unless your brother-in-law owns a collection agency and owes you a favor, you really have no practical way to enforce collection of that money. So if you tell a client or potential client that you're going to charge them for a missed appointment all you're going to do is irritate them and lose any chance for repeat business or referrals, and you're still going to be out the money.

Unrepairable computers

One of the more unfortunate situations that you'll face as a computer tech is when you have to tell somebody, "I'm sorry, but there's just nothing I can do to fix your computer." This is often a case of a bad motherboard on an older computer. In these cases it's often simply not worth it to fix the computer. I've found the best way to approach people in this situation is to tell them roughly how much it would cost to replace the motherboard. When people hear the price they usually say, "I could buy a new computer for not much more money than that," and they're right.

Another method I use to soften the blow is to point out that because of advances in technology and a drop in prices, a new machine will not only cost less than the one they're replacing did, but it will be far superior and much faster than the old one.

So although it can be a bit tricky to explain to a client that you can't repair their computer, if you approach it right most people handle the news well.

When you're not going to repair a computer, it would appear that your chance to make any money is gone, but don't despair. There is still a lot of opportunity to earn money from this client. Many people aren't comfortable buying a new computer without help. The technology and terminology confuse them, and they need someone to explain. That's you. I've actually gone on computer-buying trips with clients, visiting one or more stores to advise them on their purchase. There's good money in this, because you're getting paid for the time traveling to the stores as well as the time in the stores. Alternately, some people will buy a computer over the phone or on the Internet, and again, they'll need your advice. Many times people have asked me to make the phone calls to a computer seller or get on the Internet to place the order. Again, people are uncomfortable with the process of buying and need your help. Helping clients buy a new computer can be a lucrative part of your business.

Even after your client buys the new computer, your money-making opportunities aren't over. Most people will ask you to set up their new machine and transfer files from the old one. For me, setting up new computers was both an enjoyable and profitable aspect of my business.

Should you build and sell your own computers? I used to do this, buying the parts and the software and building a machine from scratch. But it became impossible for me, as a small business, to compete with the big boys. I couldn't match the price of a multi-national corporation that buys parts and builds computers by the thousands. So instead, when a client needed a new computer I either helped them buy online or went with them to a physical store.

Difficult people

You already know that people can be difficult to get along with. Most of the time, you just ignore or laugh off difficult people, but when you're in business, it's different. You have to work with people, no matter how difficult to get along with they may be.

I remember one client who I was meeting for the first time. Our appointment was for 8 a.m. at his office. I usually don't set appointments quite that early, but that was the time he wanted. The clock in my car read 8:01 as I parked, and my phone rang. It was my client, saying, with some impatience, "Joe, I'm waiting."

He was actually a nice guy and became a steady client whose computers I serviced for years, both in his office and at his house, but that gives you an idea of how demanding some people can be.

A surprising number of people will call and expect you to come over immediately, as in right now. Apparently it doesn't occur to them that you have other clients and other business to conduct, because they're disappointed that you aren't able to see them immediately.

What you have to do is just grin and bear it when people are rude, unpleasant or demanding. Remember, the customer isn't always right, but he or she is always the customer.

What should I charge and how much can I make?

One of the first decisions that you are going to have to make as you start your business is how you are going to charge your clients, and how much you are going to charge them. There are a couple of methods of charging clients, both with their advantages and disadvantages.

Some computer techs charge a flat rate, period. If you go this route, you will charge the same rate for the same job no matter how long the job takes to do. For example, you might charge a certain amount to replace a video card, including the part, and a larger amount to reformat a hard drive. The advantage of a flat rate for that customer is that he or she will know up front how much the job will cost. The advantage for you in a flat rate is that you will not need add up your hours to know what to charge the client in each case. There is no math involved, no figuring up your time, no decisions to make whatsoever. Both you and the client know up front exactly what the final total will be.

As far as disadvantages, for you the disadvantage is that the job may take longer than you expected. You might end up spending more hours to reformat the hard drive, including reinstalling all the customer's original files and software, than you had anticipated. It's frustrating to spend a lot of time on a job and end up not making very much per hour.

For the customer, the disadvantage of a flat rate is that he or she might pay you quite a bit of money for job that didn't take very long. The customer then feels cheated. This, in turn, is a disadvantage for you because if the customer feels cheated he or she will not have you back again for another job, nor will he or she recommend you to other potential clients.

Now let's take a look at charging by the hour. You can simply tell people "I charge X number of dollars per hour." A per hour charge can make some people wary because they know it's open-ended. People realize that computers are finicky machines and it's difficult to estimate how long it will take to fix one. People often ask "How long will this take?" and that's a tricky question. I usually tried to give them a ballpark figure, but it's difficult to know just how long many repairs will take. I didn't like to give a definite figure because if the job took longer than I said it would, and therefore cost more than the customer expected, the customer wasn't going to be happy. But you do have to answer their question, and the best you can do is give them a rough idea. For you, the advantage in charging by the hour is that the more time and effort the job takes the more money you make. You get paid for all the work you do.

Unfortunately, this is not a hard and fast rule. With computers being what they are you will run into many problems that keep you from repairing the machine quickly. Viruses and spyware, in particular, can cause you to have to spend many hours working on a computer. And the unfortunate reality is you can't always charge the client for every hour that you worked on their computer. Your charge would simply get to be too high. You might end up with $300 worth of work on a computer that's only worth $400. Clearly, if you want to be ethical, if you want repeat business, if you want referrals, you can't charge that client $300. Get used to the idea up front that you're not always going to make your usual hourly rate.

So, with both a flat rate and per-hour charge having advantages and disadvantages, I recommend you use a combination. There are certain jobs, such as replacing a bad video card, where a flat rate works great. You know how much you can buy the card for and you also know roughly how long it will take to replace it, assuming there are no other problems. So you can easily set a flat rate for replacing the card, knowing that you're being fair to your customer as well as to yourself. Keep in mind, though, that rarely - probably more like never - does a job get done without the customer saying something like, "While you're here, can you tell me how to transfer photos from my camera to the computer?" Most of the time, answers to these additional questions are short and easy. For example, someone may ask, "Can you tell me how to get rid of this icon on my desktop that I don't use?" At other times though, customers will ask questions that would take quite a long time to answer. Then what do you do? You've already told the customer what your flat-rate fee is. Perhaps he's already even paid you. The last thing you want is to spend another 20 minutes in their home without getting paid for that time. So what do you do? I think the best answer is to say, truthfully, that you have other appointments and ask if you can come back another time to teach them what they want to know. Not everyone will agree to let you do that, because they know it will cost them more money, but at least you've gotten yourself out of the sticky situation of providing free advice for 20 minutes.

Even if you use a flat rate at times, I still recommend you mostly charge by the hour. Most of the time you just don't know how long the job will take, and in those cases you should charge by the hour. A good example is when somebody calls you and says "My computer is running very slowly." There could be any number of problems causing this issue and you would not be fair to yourself to charge a flat rate in this case. Tell the client you charge X number of dollars per hour and go fix the problem as efficiently as you can. As your business begins to grow you'll soon learn when to charge by the hour and when to charge a flat rate. You'll learn what works for you, your conscience, and your clients.

How much will you charge?

Now let's tackle the difficult issue of how much to charge. Let me say up front that I am not going to tell you how much I charged, nor will I even suggest an hourly charge for you. There are several reasons that I can't tell you how much to charge. One is that rates vary widely throughout the country, depending on many factors. If there's a lot competition in your part of the country your rate is going to have to be lower. But if you live in an expensive area then your rate will have to be higher.

Another reason I can't tell you how much to charge is that I don't know when you will read this book. Like a lot of prices, the price of computer services is constantly changing. Usually they go up, but sometimes they go down as competition increases or the economy changes. Even if I could tell you how much to charge today, that price could be outdated by the time you read this book.

The third reason I won't tell you how much I charge is that I don't want to affect your decision. If I gave you a dollar figure you could easily be misled into charging too much or too little, because there are many factors that determine how much you can charge where you live.

Find out what the competition is doing

To set your rates you are going to have to get an idea of what your competition charges. There are couple of ways to do this. Let's talk about the easy one first. Visit some computer sales and repair stores and you will see that some of them list their rates in large banners behind the desk or on sheets of paper on the desk where people bring their computers. In this case it's easy to see what other places charge. I don't think that most places will like it if you get out a notepad and start writing down dollar figures, but you can unobtrusively note what they charge and then write down that information when you get to your car.

Now, the other way of finding out what other establishments charge is a bit more difficult. What you'll need to do is call computer repair people who you see advertised and ask them what they charge. I think, however, that if you simply call and say, "I'm thinking about starting a computer service and repair business and would like to know what you charge," you won't get much information. You really can't blame people for not wanting to tell you what they charge if you're going to be a competitor. Even if they give you information, it may not be accurate, and that would do you more harm than good.

Therefore, you're going to have to be a bit underhanded. I'll tell you up front I don't really like doing this and I really don't feel comfortable suggesting it, but it has to be done.

You'll have to call people and pretend you're a prospective client and then ask what they charge. I don't like the idea of deception. If you've read this book this far you know how strongly I feel about being upfront, honest, and trustworthy. However, it is critical that you do find out what your perspective competition charges and this is the only way I can think of to do that. If it makes you feel any better, I'm as certain as I can be that the same thing happened to me. I had people call and ask me what I charge to make certain repairs. I gave them an answer, they said thank you, and I never heard from them again. I had the feeling, although I can't prove it, that these were not potential clients, but potential competitors. Of course, I had no choice but to answer their question honestly and accurately because I didn't know for sure whether I was talking to a client or a competitor.

I'd suggest you get rates from at least four or five competitors. Then you have some information by which to set your own rates. I'm going to recommend that you set your rates somewhere in the middle. You don't want to be the least expensive repair person in your part of a country, because then you're cheating yourself out of income. Neither do you want to be the most expensive tech, because you won't get as much business if your prices are too much higher than your competitors.

What I'd suggest you do is set up a spreadsheet listing the names of the competitors in the first column, and then columns for where their ad ran, a trip charge, if any, first hour rate, second hour rate, and comments. In my experience, this is the information that your competitors will tell you about their charges. If you're wondering what a "second hour rate" is, some techs charge a certain amount for their first hour and a different, lower, charge for the second hour. Most, however, charge the same for the second and subsequent hours as they do for the first. You need a place for comments on your spreadsheet because some of your potential competitors will give you flat rates for certain jobs or otherwise give you information that does not fit into any certain slot. Some people charge current clients less than new clients, for example.

I would also suggest that your spreadsheet include a column for averages. You know that a spreadsheet makes it easy to average the rates that you've got from your competitors. Use that average as a guideline to set your own hourly charge.

Once you call your competitors and get their pricing information, you can start thinking about setting your own rates. It can be difficult to set your hourly rate to be fair to yourself and your clients as well as keep within the range of your competitors. But one thing to keep in mind is that your rate is never set in stone. You can lower or raise it as needed. You can charge some clients more, some clients less. You can even charge the same clients different amounts depending on the situation. If the client gives you a ton of referrals, for example, you might want to lower your rates for that client a bit. Of course, you want to tell the client you're doing that as a way of thanking them for their referrals and repeat business. That's a good business practice and one that many businesses, not only service businesses, use. For example, you've seen solicitations where current customers are offered $10 off their next purchase if they refer a new client to the business.

Remember that you are in business for yourself. You can set your rates where *you* want to, consistent with your goals of maximizing your income and keeping your clients satisfied.

How an easy problem can create a difficult one

There is another issue that often arises in this matter how much to charge people. What happens when you go to somebody's home and it takes you no time at all to determine what the problem with a computer is? You will be amazed how many times, for example, you walk into a home and spot the problem with the computer within a minute. Somebody might tell you, "I can't get my computer to start. No matter how many times I push the start button nothing happens." So quite naturally you look at the back of the computer to see if the power cord is plugged in firmly, and you find the power cord is loose. Or perhaps you notice that the computer's power strip has not been turned on. This happens even when you suggest on the phone that they check these things before you come to their home. So you plug in the power cord or press the switch on the power strip and the computer boots up normally and works just fine.

Now what do you do? Is it fair to charge somebody for an hour's labor when you worked a minute or two at the most? On the other hand, you made the journey to their home and you deserve compensation for that. So here's what I did. In these cases I charged a "trip charge." A trip charge in this case means that you're charging somebody for the trip to their home and nothing else. Your trip charge might be anywhere from $25 on up, depending on far you had to travel and what your relationship to this particular client is. For example, say you have a longtime client who lives five minutes from your home. You walk into their house and immediately spot the problem. Remember that you want to keep this person as a client and you want to keep them happy so they will recommend other people to you. I think it would be a mistake to charge this client a lot of money when they've been a good client to you over the years and not much effort on your part was involved in solving their problem. So charge them a small trip charge in this case. That way the client stays happy and yet you are compensated for your time and expertise.

My trip charge varied according to the situation. In the example I just mentioned with a longtime client who lived close to my home I might literally have not charged any more than $25. But if I had to travel farther or I spent more than just a couple minutes at the home then I might have raised that charge to perhaps $35 or more. Remember, my long term goal was to keep the client happy so that they would keep coming back to me and refer other people to me.

Now here's another variation on the scenario of going to somebody's home and finding little or nothing wrong with their computer. It might be a good idea at times to suggest to the client that you spend some more time looking over their machine, giving it a tune-up. That is, making sure their anti-virus and anti-spyware protection is up to date, making sure their operating system software is up to date, and otherwise checking their computer out and making sure it's running efficiently. Doing this work might take anywhere from 20 minutes to an hour. If it takes an hour, or close to an hour, then there's no problem. You simply charge them your usual hourly rate. If the total time you spend at their house is, say, 30 minutes, then you might decide to charge them for the entire hour or might charge them some percentage of your hourly rate. Again, your decision will depend on a number of factors, such as your relationship with a client, whether they are new or old clients, and how far you had to travel. Your decision may also depend on how many other people they referred to you in the past and therefore, the times they might refer people to you in the future. Remember, and I cannot overemphasize this point, your ultimate goal is *not* to make as much money on a particular repair as you can. Your ultimate goal is to get repeat business and referrals, because that is by far the best kind of business to get.

The trip charge revisited

Now, let's back up from moment to this idea of a trip charge. As I said earlier, it's a good idea to call some of your competitors, or potential competitors if you're new to the business, to find out what they charge. You will probably find that some of them charge a "trip charge." A trip charge can mean one of two things. It could mean that they are charging a certain amount of money, in addition to their hourly rate, just for making the trip to somebody's house. In that case, say they charge $50 an hour and also a $20 trip charge. They are actually charging $70 for that first hour. Then they charge $50 an hour after that. But what other people mean by a trip charge is a situation where there's nothing they can do to fix the computer, or the problem is solved within just a few minutes. In that case, the trip charge is a relatively small amount they charge just for coming to the house. The tech doesn't want to charge for an hour's work when he's been there 10 minutes, so he tells the customer "You only have to pay a trip charge." But if the tech is there for more than a few minutes, then the trip charge becomes irrelevant. The client is not charged a trip charge and just pays the hourly rate. This, as I said earlier, is the practice I followed.

I don't think it's wise to charge a trip charge in addition to your usual hourly rate. I think the client would resent that extra charge and therefore not be happy with you as a service provider. And I'll repeat it once again, if you want to succeed in this business you must keep your clients happy. You cannot succeed without referrals and repeat business. So once again, what you want is a set of charges that is fair to both to you and your client. My experience was that clients were delighted when all I charged them was a trip charge when I was only at their house for a few minutes. And a delighted client is a client who will have you back to their home or business again.

What to do when someone asks you to lower your usual rate

I didn't have this happen a ton of times, but on occasion someone flat out asked me if I could do a job for less than my usual fee. Sometimes people pled poverty. They said something like, "I don't have very much money right now," and sometimes I could see by their circumstances that they were probably telling the truth. So, do you stick to your guns and charge your usual fee, or do you offer to do the job for bit less money? My practice was to lower my rate when I thought it prudent to do so. It again comes down to the matter of good customer relations leading to more business. Think of it this way: would you rather have one hour of work at say, $10 or $15 less than you usually make an hour, or would you rather have a no hours of work at all? To me, it was a no-brainer. I'd take less than my usual rate rather than not make any money at all. Think about what you'll do in this situation, because it will arise at some time and you want to be able to answer a client or potential client.

Service contracts

Some computer repair businesses sell service contracts, which is when a client pays X amount of dollars and, in return, gets the services of the technician for a specified time period. Contract terms vary widely. Sometimes the contract provides unlimited free service over the life of the contract; other times the contract states that the client will receive discount pricing. Or the contract may call for the service person to make a least one call per year to the client at no additional charge.

I never used service contracts. I thought my clients, who are mostly older people, might have found them confusing and/or intimidating. And there's an old rule in business, "A confused mind never buys." In short, I think service contracts might hurt more than help you earn more money.

There are legal and practical issues with service contracts, too. To be done right, you should get an attorney's help in drawing up a service contract, which is, after all, a legal document. And, as you know, attorneys can be expensive. You might have to sell a lot of service contracts to offset the money you spend having it drawn up.

Also, what happens if you get sick or injured and you're contractually required to make service calls? You may have to refund the money clients paid or pay someone else to make the calls for you.

Some say service contracts are a good way to supplement your income, and you might want to try using them. Just be aware of the pitfalls I've mentioned.

Potential earnings

How much can you make in this business? Obviously, that depends on how much business you can round up. In fact, that's a disadvantage to owning and running a service business. Generally speaking, you can only make money while you're actually working.

As you know, a standard work week is 40 hours. You know, of course, that being in business for yourself probably means that you will be working more than 40 hours per week. But remember that you will not be able to work 40 *billable* hours per week. For a start, in a computer service business, you must allow for travel time. What I found is that on average I had to allow about 1/2 hour travel time for every billable hour. So if you're working a 40 hour week, you actually only have about 27 billable hours. But in reality, you may have even less than 27 billable hours. You must allow time for buying parts, record keeping, and as I mentioned earlier, sometimes you simply cannot charge a customer for all the hours you may have worked on a computer. So for a 40 hour work week you'll probably have about 20 to 25 billable hours. Multiply those 20-plus hours by your hourly charge and that's about what you can earn per week. For example: 20 hours times $60 an hour equals $1,200 a week.

Then multiply that figure by 50 weeks to get your total possible earnings for the year. I say 50 weeks because I recommend that you will allow some time for vacations, and also because there are certain days in the year that you probably will not be working, such as the six major holidays. So, then, 50 weeks times $1,200 a week equals $60,000 a year.

If that sounds good to you, remember there are many reasons why that won't be your actual income per year. There will be some weeks when you will not have 20 or more billable hours, because you just don't have enough clients call for your services. Also, depending on what part of the country you live in, there may be some days when you can't work because of weather conditions. Keep in mind that your earnings, then, will fluctuate from week to week.

Expenses

In any business, you're going to have a fair amount of expenses, and the computer repair business is no different. The greatest expense (except for parts, which customers will reimburse you for) will be advertising. You also have to do a far amount of driving to your appointments, and gas can be a big expense. Then there are taxes. As a self-employed person, you not only have to pay income tax like anyone else, you also have to pay both sides of the Social Security and Medicare taxes. You may know that when you work as an employee your employer pays half your Social Security and Medicare taxes. The amount you pay every week (currently about seven percent of your pay) is only half of the total Social Security and Medicare tax. Your employer pays an equal amount to the federal government on your behalf. But when you're self-employed you pay the entire amount yourself. So that potential $60,000 a year quickly becomes considerably less.

Because you can't count on a certain amount of income every week, it helps a lot if you have a spouse working a regular job so you can count on his or her income every week. And it's also a great help if your spouse has health insurance through his or her job. If your spouse has health insurance at work you'll pay far less for this essential coverage than if you have to buy it yourself. If you do have to buy your own health insurance, be prepared to pay a *lot* for it.

Record keeping

As you begin your business you'll quickly find that it's important to keep complete and accurate records of your business dealings. There are many reasons for this, not the least of which is that good records will help you do your job efficiently. The last thing you want is to lose a client's address or phone number. You'll also need good records for tax purposes.

To keep my records, I had a spreadsheet named with four tabs - clients, mileage, expenses, and newsletter.

Let's look at these tabs one by one. The client tab was, of course, a list of all my clients. It contained columns for an e-mail address, name, phone number, address, city, zip code, number of sessions I had with that client, number of hours with them, hourly rate, total money, and comments

I usually didn't ask clients for their e-mail address, but if I happened to see it, I'd try to remember it and make a note of it when I got to the car. And of course my e-mail address was on my business card and when people sent me e-mails I'd have their address. I rarely sent e-mail to clients for the obvious reason: we get too much e-mail as it is and I didn't want to offend a client by sending them unsolicited e-mail. But at times having clients' e-mail addresses comes in handy. Say, for example, that a virulent new virus arises. It probably wouldn't hurt to send an e-mail to your clients letting them know about it. Doing so doesn't cost you anything but a few minutes of your time, and most people will appreciate that you're trying to keep their computer from getting a virus and you just might get an appointment or two from sending the e-mail. So, in retrospect, I think now I should have asked each client for their e-mail address. I could have used the same logic I just mentioned - "Sometimes I send my clients an email about potential threats to computers. Do you mind if I get your email address? I promise I won't send you a lot of unsolicited emails." I believe that few, if any, of my clients would have refused.

The "name," "phone number," "address," "city," and "zip code" columns on the spreadsheet are self explanatory. The "number of sessions" column told me how many times I'd been to that clients' home or business. I kept that information because I found it useful to know who my best clients were. The "number of hours" column told me how many hours I spent at the client's home or business, and again, this was useful to me in knowing who my most active clients were. The "hourly rate" column told me what I charged that particular client per hour. The hourly rate can vary between clients for several reasons. One is that you might raise your rates, but not wish to pass that raise on to some current clients. You might also decide to charge a particular client more or less than your current usual rate. For example, if a client is outside your normal business area you might charge them more per hour to help pay for the time it takes you to get to that home or business. Or maybe you have a client who clearly is not well off financially and you decide to charge that person a little less per hour than normal, figuring, as I did, that it's better to have a client at $10 less an hour than my usual rate than to not have a client at all.

The "total" column contained a formula. The formula multiplied the "number of hours" and "hourly rate" columns to tell me the total amount of money I had made from that client. And the "comments" column could have contained any number of different types of useful information, such as the fact that this client was a referral from another client.

The next tab on my spreadsheet was the mileage tab. You absolutely must keep track of your mileage for tax purposes. When you file your taxes you will be able to deduct the actual mileage you traveled on business. The IRS will tell you each year how much you can deduct per business mile traveled. Currently the amount is 56 cents per mile for business miles, but the rate usually goes up every year. You will multiply the number of business miles that you traveled by the current mileage rate and deduct this amount from your gross business income. This will save you a lot of money in taxes. The "mileage" tab on my spreadsheet contained columns for the date, trip purpose, starting mileage, end mileage and total miles. You'll also need a column that lists any tolls you may have had to pay. Tolls, like mileage, are deductible from your gross income.

I cannot overstress to you the importance of keeping a mileage log. You must do this in order to deduct your business mileage from your taxes, and your records must be pretty much as mine were to be acceptable to the IRS.

The third tab on my business spreadsheet was called "expenses," and this is another critically important record for you to keep. This tab on my spreadsheet was very simple. It had just three columns - one for the type of expense, one for the date, and one for the amount of the expense.

The final tab on my business spreadsheet was one I called "newsletter." This tab will be optional for you. You'll recall that I suggested earlier and that you send a newsletter to your current clients to keep your name before them. If you do that, I suggest you keep a spreadsheet tab with the names and addresses of all the clients you send a newsletter to. All your clients will not necessarily receive a newsletter, but what you can do is copy and paste your client list to this newsletter tab and then delete any clients' names who you decide not to send a newsletter to. I used the mail merge feature in a word processing program to print my clients' names and addresses on envelopes for the newsletter.

You probably won't want to copy my recordkeeping system exactly. More than likely, you'll come up with a system that works for you. But make sure you do use some kind of system to accurately keep track of your business records. Sure, recordkeeping takes time, and that's time that you're not using to actually make money. But it has to be done, so develop a system that's efficient, accurate, and user friendly.

Taxes

Let me preface this section by stating that I am not an accountant or a tax lawyer. You should rely on your tax professional when submitting your tax returns. But here are a few basics to get you started.

As a self-employed computer technician and business owner, you'll need to report your writing income and expenses to the Internal Revenue Service. You'll use Schedule C to report both your income and expenses. If your state has an income tax, you'll need to report your income to the state as well.

As I mentioned earlier, you can deduct your expenses from your gross income. Some expenses you may be able to deduct are:

Advertising

The cost of parts

The business portion of your cell phone charges

Computer software

Tools

Postage and the cost of copying your newsletter, if you send one to your clients

Mileage to and from business appointments

You *may* also be able to deduct a portion of the cost of your personal computer and be able to take the home office deduction. Check with a tax attorney or accountant on these matters.

Be sure to get and save receipts for all expenses. You'll need them to file your taxes.

Remember that you will be responsible for paying income taxes on your net profit. You also must pay both sides of your social security tax and Medicare, which alone are quite a large chunk out of your gross income.

The amount of federal income tax you pay depends on your tax bracket, but will again be a large bite of your income.

As a self-employed individual you won't have taxes withheld from your pay, so you may need to make quarterly tax payments to the IRS. Each payment should be one-fourth of the total taxes you expect to owe that year. The trouble is, it's impossible to know how much money you'll make in a particular year, and hence how much you'll owe in taxes. Your best bet is to pay one-fourth of *last year's* tax bill. As long as you pay 100 percent of your previous year's taxes, you won't owe a penalty to the IRS, even if you end up owing money at the end of the tax year.

When you file your tax return, you'll need to complete Schedule C (Profit or Loss from Business) and Schedule SE (Self-Employment Tax).

Appendix 1: Useful web sites

There are a number of web sites you will find useful in running your business. These sites are for you, not necessarily for your clients. Web sites, of course, come and go. These addresses were accurate at the time of writing.

driverguide.com

This is a useful web site when you are reformatting a hard drive. Much of the time you will find that the client does not have the software to reinstall the drivers for the video card, Ethernet card, or sound card. If Windows can't install the driver what you can do is get the model number of the individual cards and go to driverguide.com to get the necessary drivers. This site contains thousands of drivers and I rarely found that I wasn't able to find a driver for a particular card at the site.

housecall.trendmicro.com

This site contains a free anti-virus scanning program. You'll find this useful when a client has a computer with a stubborn virus problem. In addition to running and rerunning what ever anti-virus program they may have on the computer I suggest you go to this site and run their anti-virus check on the computer.

www.crucial.com

This is a site to go to buy memory. Find the make and model number of the computer and crucial.com will tell you exactly what memory that computer takes. You can then order that memory right from the site and have it delivered in a very short period of time. It may be possible to buy memory at other places on the Internet besides crucial.com for less money, but I don't know of any place that provides the service that crucial does, both in telling you exactly what memory you need and in delivering the item quickly.

www.pcguide.com

This is a very useful educational site. If you are new to the computer service business, or even if you're not, you'll learn a lot about servicing computers by browsing this site.

zip4.usps.com

If you follow my advice in the advertising section and send a newsletter periodically to your clients you will probably need this site to look up zip codes for some of your clients. Usually you can get the zip code off the check the client pays you with, but some clients pay with cash and others won't have their address, or at least not their current address, on their checks. You can easily find zip codes at this website.

www.download.com

As its name implies, this website provides a place for you to download computer software. Some of the software is free, some is shareware, and some is commercial software. But you'll find a lot of useful software at download.com. Another useful site for finding software is www.nonags.com.

There are also numerous web sites that sell computer parts and supplies. There are far too many to mention, and besides, the sites constantly change, so I won't list specific sites. Just do a search for "computer parts" and you'll find plenty of places online to buy parts, often for less money than you will find locally. Just be careful about quality.

Appendix 2: Anti-virus and other security software

Always do your clients the favor of making sure where they have up to date anti-virus and anti-spyware programs installed on their computers so they are fully protected from the scourges of the Internet. You can make money by installing these programs and also by showing your clients how to run them. In fact, some clients will ask you to run the programs because they just won't know how to, despite your instructions. I recommend Avast as a free anti-virus program, and Ad-Aware, Malwarebytes, and Spybot as anti-spyware programs.

Another enemy for those who surf the Internet is popup ads. Should you install a popup stopper for your clients? As you probably know, popup stoppers can be a problem in that they sometimes stop legitimate web sites or Windows from appearing. You also probably know there's an easy way around that problem, which is usually to hold down the control or shift key, which allows the window to appear that the popup stopper otherwise would have stopped. That sounds easy for me or for you to do, but for many clients that would be difficult, if not impossible. For a start they would forget which key they were supposed to hold down if they had a problem with a window not appearing. And for many clients holding down the shift or control key would be very confusing. I know that's probably hard to believe if you haven't had a whole lot of experience dealing with computer users, but believe me, it's true. My rather reluctant solution has been to usually stop installing popup stoppers for clients. If the client uses a computer well, I do install a popup stopper, otherwise I don't raise the issue.

Appendix 3: Having a partner

You may wonder if it's a good idea to have a business partner. The advantages are obvious. If you are busy with another repair job, or even if you just have other plans, your partner can go to a client's home or business and do the job. Meanwhile, you can still get some of the money because you have an agreement with your partner that you split the revenues no matter who does the work. A common arrangement is for each partner, assuming there are just two, to get two-thirds of the money for work that he does and one-third of the money for work that the other partner does. You can readily see that this arrangement works to the advantage of both partners. Another advantage to having a partner is that you can take a vacation without losing all your income. Furthermore, a partner is useful to when you are stumped with a problem. The partner may have seen that particular problem before and be able to show you how to handle it. You will also find that with a partner you will get more work done than two individuals working separately would get done.

Having said all that, however, I must also tell you that although I once had a business partner, I had to break off the partnership. The partnership had its origin when I met a guy about my age who also had a keen interest in computers. We hit it off immediately and soon became good friends. I had been in business about three years at the time and the time seemed right to expand by joining with somebody else. So I asked my friend to join me in my business, which he readily agreed to do. We reached an arrangement about paying for expenses and handling incoming business. For a few months all was great. I found my expenses cut in half and my income increasing. I also learned a lot from my partner, and he learned a lot from me.

Unfortunately, after a while matters began to deteriorate. I began hearing complaints from some of my regular clients. They were telling me that my partner was impatient and bordering on rude with them. I was a little surprised because my partner was a very nice guy who I got along splendidly with. But of course I knew my clients weren't telling me this just for the fun of it. They had reasons to be dissatisfied with my partner. My business partner turned out to be a guy who, although well versed in working with computers and easy for me to get along with, just didn't do well with people who had little computer knowledge. So I ended up a breaking off the partnership arrangement. Fortunately, we remained friends, but I found myself disillusioned on the partnership idea.

I'm not telling you not to have a partner. In fact, I am saying that a partner can be of great help to you and your business. But it can be difficult to find just the right person to work with. You're probably better off with someone you've already known for a long time, instead of partnering with someone you've known just for a few months, as I did.

I don't think any real long term damage was done by my taking on a partner, but there might have been. If you can find the right person to partner up with, go for it.

Printed in Great Britain
by Amazon

79130088R10034